300

THE HOFFNUNG MUSIC FESTIVAL

The *Hoffnung* Music Festival

Per Tuba ad Astra.

by

Gerard Hoffnung

LONDON

DOBSON · PUTNAM

First published September 1956
Reprinted February 1957
Reprinted November 1957
Reprinted November 1958

To
The Morley College Symphony Orchestra
and its inspired conductor Lawrence
Leonard, with much affection.

The Conductors

Alerto

Preciso

Con adornamento

Grandioso

Agilmente

Piano

Con fuoco

Senza batone

Slargando

Maestoso

Non troppo

Elegantemente

Sehr markiert

Sotto

Bel Canto

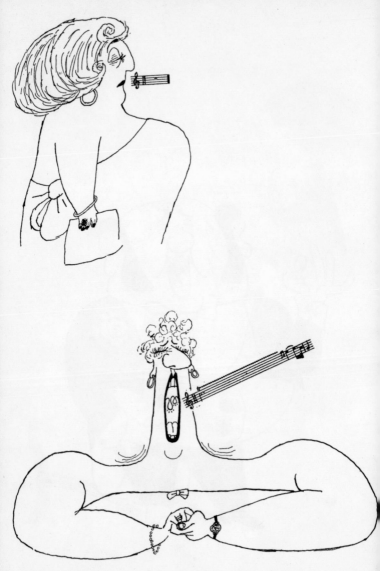

Coloratura

Basso

Signorina...
acknowledges
applause

A sextet

The Festival Chorus

The Soloists

T.V. brings
the Festival
to a wider
audience

An unfortunate incident

Mainly
Instrumental

The
Trout Quintet

VACUUM QUARTET IN A FLAT
(THE HOOVER)

for
two vacuums in **f**
one vacuum in E flat*
one contra vacuum in BB flat
(World première)

*If desired this may be replaced by an
electric Floor-polisher in A flat.

Con Sord *

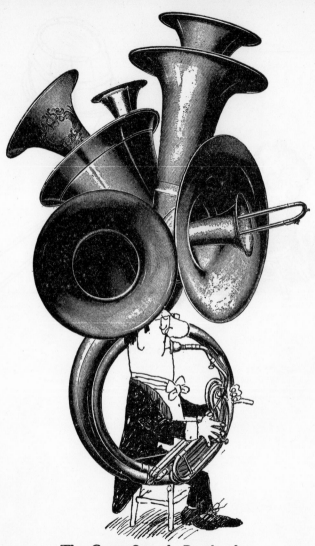

The Great Octuple Bombardon
(Americano Expresso)

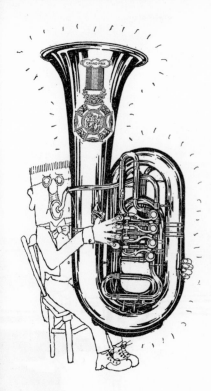

Tuba alla Tedesca

Tuba Anglais
(Leeds)

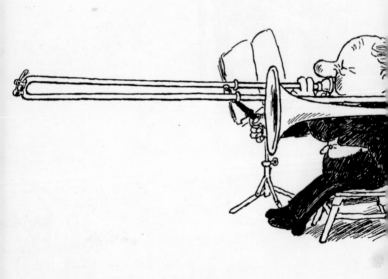

THE END